Choose a topic and start to practise writing. Each booklet has a theme to help you start to write…stories, reports, articles, letters and many more. Start collecting them now.

Guinea Pig creative writing booklets also provide extra practice for children who have completed:

- Creative Story Writing ISBN: 9780955831508
- Persuasive Writing & Argument ISBN: 9780955831515
- Information Writing ISBN: 9780955831522

They are for:

* children who are working at Key Stage 2 of the National Curriculum, levels 3-5 (in Years 5 and 6 of primary school),
* children who are working at Key Stage 3, levels 3-5 (Years 7 and 8 of Secondary School).

They provide practice for all 9-13 year olds, especially children taking 11+ examinations.

Let's **learn** to *write* <u>non-fiction</u>.

When you *write non-fiction*, <u>**you may write**</u>:

- an article

- a leaflet

- a diary

- a description.

> - *A description may describe the way people look, dress, their character, attitudes and abilities.*
> - *A description may describe the way a place looks.*
> - *A description may describe the way something feels, tastes and smells.*

<u>You must decide</u>:

1. Who will be my target audience?

2. Who will read this writing?

3. What is the purpose of my writing?

4. Am I aiming to give somebody a picture of something I have experienced?

5. Am I using my senses to impact the reader- seeing, hearing, feeling, touching, tasting?

<u>Use imagery or figurative language:</u>

Metaphors - *'princely paper.'*

Similes - *'feeling like a princess.'*

Personification - *'the rustling paper whispers softly.'*

Admirable adjectives and nouns - *'mysterious parcel.'*

Powerful verbs and adverbs - *'rummage eagerly.'*

When you write to **describe**:

PARAGRAPH 1 • Write an introduction to set the scene. • Have a colourful opening to get the attention of the reader.	**Remember:** • Use powerful words - verbs, adverbs, nouns and adjectives. • Use similes and metaphors.
PARAGRAPH 2, 3, 4... • Write about each part of this experience in separate paragraphs - in the best order.	• Use connectives or conjunctions: - *and or but (to join compound sentences)* - *or, so, if, when, while, after, before, because, unless, until, whereas, although (to join complex sentences)* - *use pronouns - who, which, whose, what, that* - *to link ideas use - firstly, later, therefore, on the other hand, at that moment, by this time, next, soon...* • Use a range of sentences – simple, compound and complex sentences
Conclusion • Draw all your ideas together in a conclusion.	• Make personal comments

The **Present**

The mysterious parcel is shaped like a box. It is covered in luxurious, multi-coloured wrapping paper and waits for me on the table. It looks majestic. The shiny paper glitters, sending particles of silver light dancing playfully across the carpet. A large, impressive bow perches magnificently on the top. Layers of folded ribbon cascade down the side like a waterfall. The wrapped gift looks amazing. It fills me with curiosity. My eyes are drawn towards it as it seems to shout, "Look at me! Aren't I splendid?" Then, I start to anticipate what lies beneath the ostentatious (rich) exterior. I tentatively feel the box for clues but the tension is mounting. I hear excited cries,
"Open it! Open it!"

My excited fingers caress the shimmering outer wrap and fumble to untie the ribbon. I rip away the princely paper. I peel back the layers of gift-wrap which I discard in shreds on the floor. Everyone in the room looks on with excitement as the box is revealed. I attempt to prise off the lid but it resists me. I tug and tug until it budges. I peer expectantly at the contents. My hands rummage eagerly through the fragile layers of pink tissue, scented with rose perfume and dotted with confetti. The rustling paper whispers softly to me as I delve deep into the layers. It crumples in my hand as I reach into the bottom of the box to discover its secret.

Ending One

My hand brushes against soft fur. I stroke what seem to be a head and two ears. I pull the ear gently towards me. A face appears from out of the box; it has a brown button nose, two black felt eyes and the cutest grin. What a surprise! Triumphantly, I hold him out for all to see. I say, "He's gorgeous. He's the cutest thing I've ever seen. Thank you so much" I hug and hug and hug my new found friend.

Ending Two

My hand grasps a sparkling jewel. It has three precious gems dangling in a cluster from a delicate chain. The crystals gleam brilliantly. I hold it to my neck proudly, imagining myself wearing it. I can hardly believe something so precious is mine.

Your turn to write.

Think about a present you have received.

- What did it look like on the table?

- How did you feel as you opened it?

- What was inside?

Use the questions on the next page to help you write a description of the day you opened it.

Structure your writing in three paragraphs. Each paragraph will be about a different part of opening the present.

1. Receiving the present, seeing it on the table

2. Opening the present

3. The contents

Use these sentences to help you write the story.

(Paragraph 1)

What do you see on the table?

What does the wrapping paper look like?

Describe the bow.

How does it make you feel and why?

What does your friend (member of the family) say?

(Paragraph 2)

How do you tear off the paper and what happens to it?

How do you tug off the lid?

When you peep inside, what do you see?

When you reach down deep into the box, what do you hear?

What do your hands feel in there?

(Paragraph 3)

What is your present?

Describe what it looks and feels like?

What do you do?

What do you say?

Here are some sentences to get you started.

The …………………………………………………………………… parcel waits

for me on the table. It looks ……………………………………………………

There is a large bow, which is perched magnificently on top. The wrapped gift looks

amazing. It makes me feel……………………………………………………………

……………………………………………………………………………………

It seems to say to me…………………………………………………………………

……………………………………………………………………………………

I start to imagine what is in the parcel. My family cry, "…………………………………

………………………………………………………………………………"

My excited fingers feel (caress) the …………………………………………………

First, I rip away at …………………………………………………………………

After this, I peel back …………………………… to reveal …………………………

……………………………………………………………………………………

The paper lies in shreds on the…………………….......……………… As my family watch, I

attempt to tear …………………………………………… I tug at ……………………

…………………………… Then, I peer into ……………………………………………

………………………………………… I delve deep in ……………………………

My hands rummage eagerly through the pink tissue paper, which smells of ……………

………………I crumple the paper in my hands, it sounds like…………….....……………

………………………………………… In my hand I feel……………………………………

…………………At last I take out …………………………………………………………

……………………………………………………………………………………

What a surprise. There is a …………………………………………………………………

……………………………………………………………………………………

……………………………………… I hold the gift out for my family to see. Afterwards, I say,

"…………………………………………………………………………………

……………………………………………………………………………………

……………………………………………………………………………………

………………………………………………………………………………"

Now write the story you planned.

Moving the story on:

Now write an imaginative story. Let your imagination work...

Everyone in our house knew that Auntie Katy chose boring presents. Don't get me wrong, it wasn't that I was ungrateful for her gifts and it wasn't that they were useless either. Far from it, they were the most useful things – like pairs of warm socks for winter days, white cotton boxer shorts or a paper pad for school. They were just run of the mill, everyday things. And so the day she dropped in with a package the size of a shoebox, I said to myself, they're a pair of black plimsolls for P.E – bought from the sale at Fresco. I undid the blue, shiny paper (that had certainly wrapped at least three other gifts) and exposed a black, shiny box. Inside was a pair of cheap, white trainers with laces.

"Thanks," I muttered. "Just what I needed," and I put them in a box in my bedroom and forgot about them.

The next week, I was tying the laces of my cool designer trainers when the lace broke. It snapped off. What should I do? I was rushing to my football club. Then, I remembered Aunty Katy's white trainers. I raced upstairs. I grabbed them from the box and put them on... and off I went. It usually took fifteen minutes to walk to the sports club where I did my training, but today it took only five. I seemed to fly along. We started the match. I was playing mid-field, but soon I took control of the ball and I kicked it straight into the goal. We kicked off again - within minutes I had scored another goal... and then another... and then another. We won 9-0. I had never shown so much skill at football. As we left the pitch my team mates were looking at me.

● Now write the third paragraph. Use the questions to help you.

- What do your team mates say?

- Are they impressed or astonished by your new talent?

- Does your team win the cup?

- How does it end?

- Was it anything to do with the trainers?

Paragraph 3

....

....

....

....

....

....

....

....

....

....

....

....

Imagine some more adventures Jacob could have wearing the trainers.

- Could he run round the world?

- Could he win a gold medal in the Olympics?

- Does word get round that these shoes are special? Do they go missing?

Write your story:

In **paragraph 1** imagine you received an unusual present:

- What was the present?
- Where were you?
- Who gave it to you?
- How did you feel?

In **paragraph 2**:

- What happened next?
- And after that?
- Then… *build up suspense as events unfold.*

In **paragraph 3**:

- Wind up the story.
- What is the resolution?
- Is it a happy ending, sad ending, cliffhanger or moral lesson learnt?

Use your <u>*imagination*</u> *to write stories.*

What type or genre of story could it be?

- a **fantasy** story… your present comes alive or transports you to another land

- a **crime** story… your present is stolen

- an **epic adventure** story… your present leads you to find something

Can you think of some more?

Now write the story you planned.

....

....

....

....

....

....

....

....

....

....

....

....

....

....

....

....

....

....

....

....

....

....

....

....

Write Jacob's thank you letter to Aunty Katy. Remember, to set out the letter with correct punctuation. Use the letter below to help you.

23 Louisville Road,

Rushford,

RG12 6AH.

Dear Aunty Katy,

Thank you so much for those white trainers you gave me. I really like them, as they are really comfortable and match my other sports wear. In fact, I wear them for all my sports sessions now. I prefer them to my designer ones.

Since I've started wearing them, I've scored so many goals in matches. Besides this, my team has done so well in the league that we're tipped to win the championship. Next week I plan to take them on my holiday, because I'll need a good pair of shoes to see the sights – The Taj Mahal, The pyramids of Egypt and the Acropolis in Athens. With these trainers it doesn't take long to get anywhere.

In fact, I was going to ask you where you got them from? My friends would all like a pair. They are all pretty envious and ask me which shop stocks them. I just said that they were a present from my aunt. Yes, these trainers are truly MAGIC! By the way do they have...

Oh mum's come in to take this letter to the post office, so I'll have to stop now.

Love from

Jac

** Note that humour is used.*

It is written in first person. It is chatty, informal and personal - to a friend. It uses present tense. It is light hearted, with a humorous tone.

Now write your reply.

Now, write a thank you letter for a present you received on your birthday.
Use these sentences to help you.

....

....

....

....

Dear ....,

Thank you for the parcel you sent me for my birthday. It arrived on ....

.... When I saw the postman .... up the path with a

.... I was so ....

....

On the day of my birthday, which was ...., I got up ....

and ....

When I opened the box you sent me, I was ....

.... because ....

The day was .... My sister bought me a ....

....

I had .... cards and ....

....

In the afternoon some friends came round and we went to ....

....

at .... It was ....

Thanks again,

Love from,

....

Look up the following words in the dictionary.

crinkle, wrinkle, **crackle**, crease, crumple, <u>fold</u>, curl, **crimp**

glitter, <u>shine</u>, dazzle, **sparkle**, **gleam**, shimmer, twinkle, glint, glimmer, *dazzle*

valuable, collectable, gift

great, *wonderful*, brilliant, stunning. <u>overwhelming</u>, incredible, astonishing, staggering, **marvellous**. <u>breathtaking</u>, awesome, **astounding**, amazing

thrilled, excited, *pleased*, happy. <u>grateful</u>

Informal language: **ace, mega**

splendid, *exciting*, <u>impressive</u>, **magnificent**

Find some more words by looking in a thesaurus. Write them on this page.

Made in the USA
Monee, IL
08 July 2026